MUSIC MADE EASY

COLLECTION

CHORDS MASTERY:
A VISUAL GUIDE IN 5 STEPS

~ Guitar Edition ~

Written by
Andrew Milner

Table of Contents

CHORDS MASTERY:
A VISUAL GUIDE IN 5 STEPS

~ Guitar Edition ~

Andrew Milner

MUSIC MADE EASY

COLLECTION

Basic Chords

Major chords

1. Consist of 3 notes;
2. Intervals between notes: M3, m3;
3. M3 = major third, m3 = minor third;
4. Ex: C is C–E–G;
5. Formula can be used on any note.

The C chord Tabs

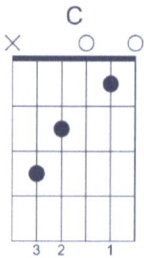

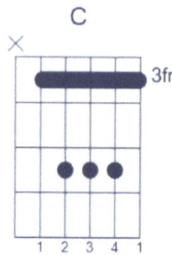

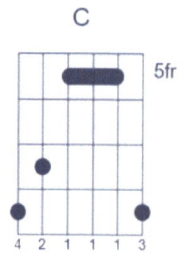

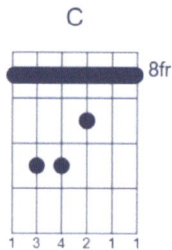

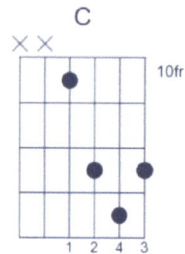

Minor chords

1. Consist of 3 notes;
2. Intervals between notes: m3, M3;
3. M3 = major third, m3 = minor third;
4. Ex: Cm is C–Eb–G;
5. Formula can be used on any note.

The Cm chord Tabs

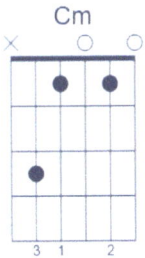

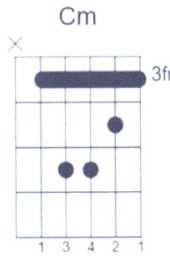

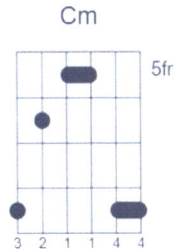

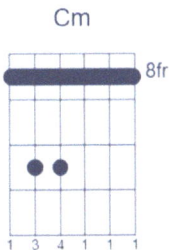

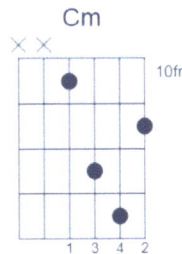

Augmented chords

1. Consist of 3 notes;
2. Intervals between notes: M3, M3;
3. M3 = major third;
4. Ex: Caug is C–E–G#;
5. Formula can be used on any note.

The Caug chord Tabs

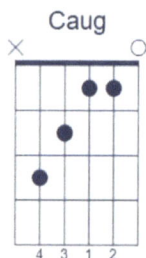

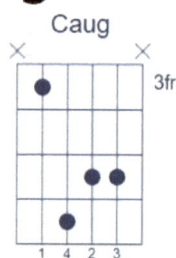

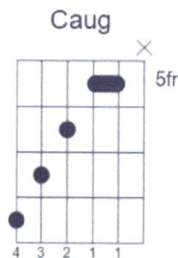

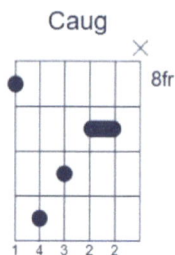

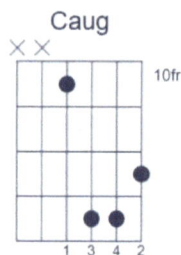

Caug

Caug

Caug

Caug

Caug

Diminished chords

1. Consist of 3 notes;
2. Intervals between notes: m3, m3;
3. m3 = minor third;
4. Ex: Cdim is C–Eb–Gb;
5. Formula can be used on any note.

The Cdim chord Tabs

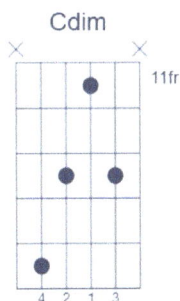

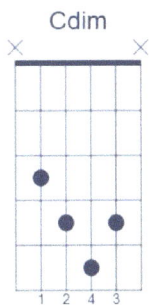

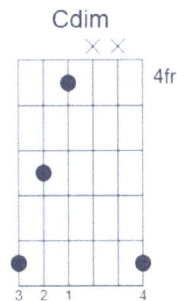

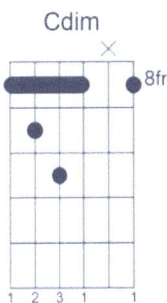

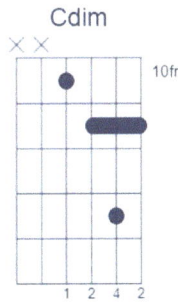

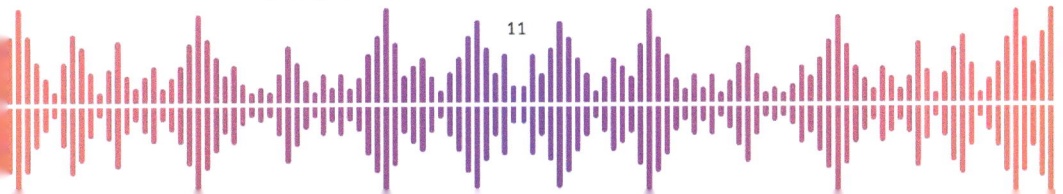

Cdim

Cdim

Cdim

Cdim

Cdim

7th Chords

Major 7th chords

1. Consist of 4 notes;
2. Intervals between notes: M3, m3, M3;
3. M3 = major third, m3 = minor third;
4. Ex: Cmaj7 is C–E–G–B;
5. Formula can be used on any note.

The Cmaj7 chord Tabs

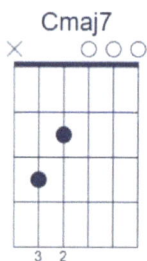

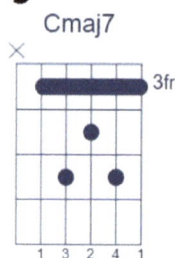

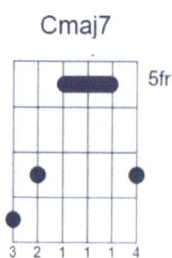

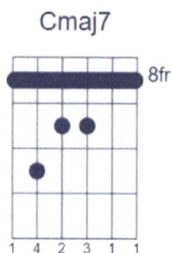

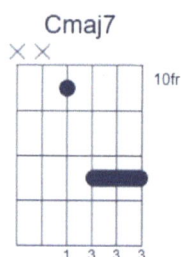

Cmaj7

Cmaj7
3fr

Cmaj7
5fr

Cmaj7
8fr

Cmaj7
10fr

Dominant 7th chords

1. Consist of 4 notes;
2. Intervals between notes: M3, m3, m3;
3. M3 = major third, m3 = minor third;
4. Ex: C7 is C–E–G–Bb;
5. Formula can be used on any note.

The C7 chord Tabs

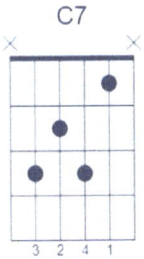

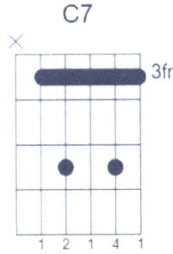

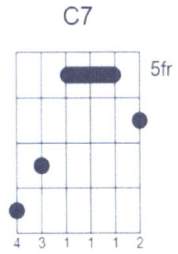

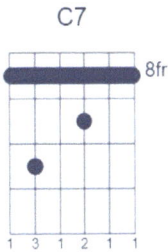

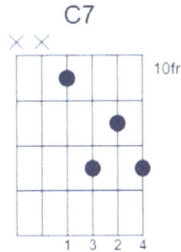

C7

× ×

3 2 4 1

C7

×

3fr

1 2 1 4 1

C7

5fr

4 3 1 1 1 2

C7

8fr

1 3 1 2 1 1

C7

× ×

10fr

1 3 2 4

Minor 7th chords

1. Consist of 4 notes;
2. Intervals between notes: m3, M3, m3;
3. M3 = major third, m3 = minor third;
4. Ex: Cm7 is C–Eb–G–Bb;
5. Formula can be used on any note.

The Cm7 chord Tabs

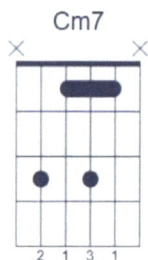

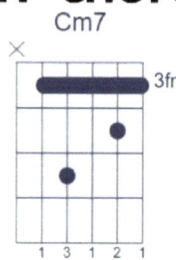

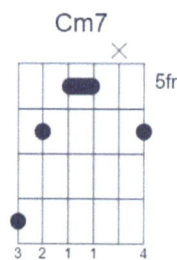

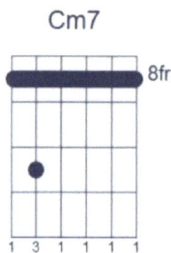

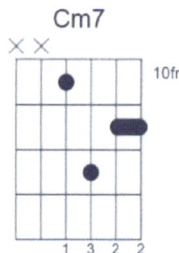

Cm7

Cm7 — 3fr

Cm7 — 5fr

Cm7 — 8fr

Cm7 — 10fr

Minor 7(b5) chords

1. Consist of 4 notes;
2. Intervals between notes: m3, m3, M3;
3. M3 = major third, m3 = minor third;
4. Ex: Cm7(b5) is C–Eb–Gb–Bb;
5. Formula can be used on any note.

The Cm7(b5) chord Tabs

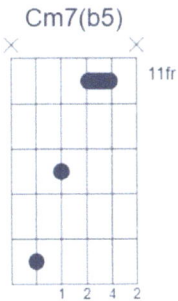

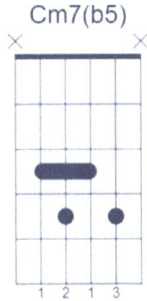

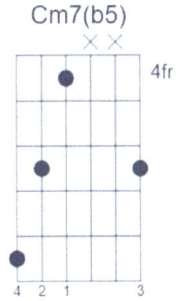

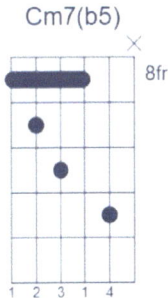

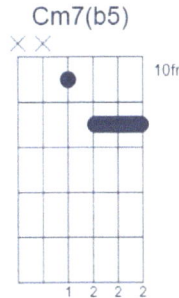

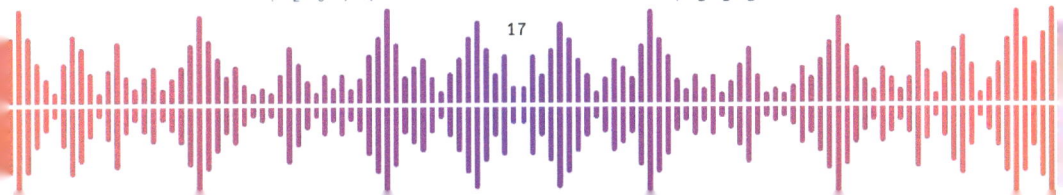

Diminished 7th chords

1. Consist of 4 notes;
2. Intervals between notes: m3, m3, m3;
3. M3 = major third, m3 = minor third;
4. Ex: Cdim7 is C–Eb–Gb–Bbb(A);
5. Formula can be used on any note.

The Cdim7 chord Tabs

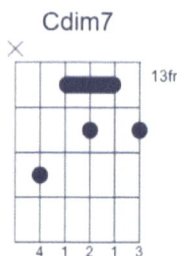

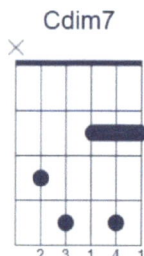

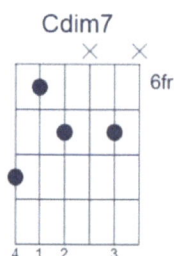

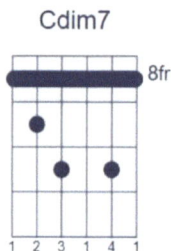

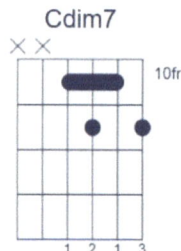

Cdim7

13fr

4 1 2 1 3

Cdim7

2 3 1 4 1

Cdim7

6fr

4 1 2   3

Cdim7

8fr

1 2 3 1 4 1

Cdim7

10fr

1 2 1 3

Suspended Chords

Sus2 chords

1. Consist of 3 notes;
2. Intervals between notes: M2, P4;
3. M2 = major second, P4 = perfect fourth;
4. Ex: Csus2 is C–D–G;
5. Formula can be used on any note.

The Csus2 chord Tabs

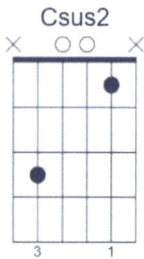

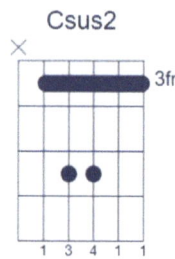

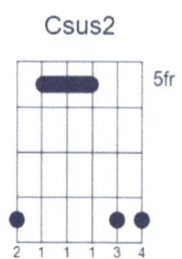

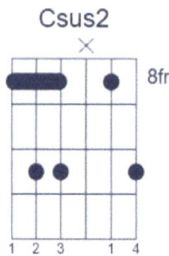

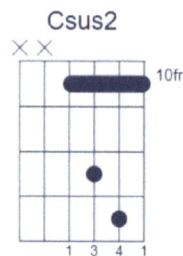

Csus2

Csus2 3fr

Csus2 5fr

Csus2 8fr

Csus2 10fr

Sus4 chords

1. Consist of 3 notes;
2. Intervals between notes: P4, M2;
3. M2 = major second, P4 = perfect fourth;
4. Ex: Csus4 is C–F–G;
5. Formula can be used on any note.

The Csus4 chord Tabs

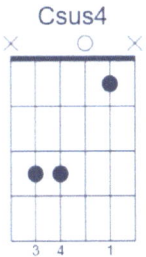

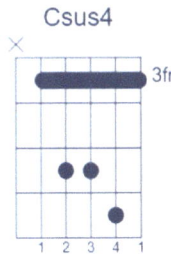

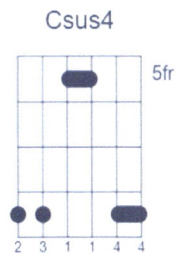

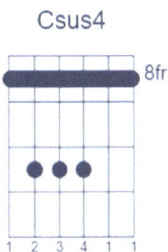

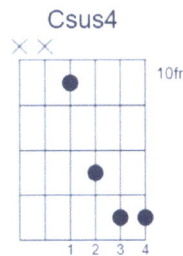

Csus4

Csus4   3fr

Csus4   5fr

Csus4   8fr

Csus4   10fr

Power Chords
and
Chord Inversions

Power chords

1. Consist of 2 notes;

2. Intervals between notes: P5;

3. P5 = perfect fifth;

4. Ex: F5 is F–C; you can add a F after C;

5. Formula can be used on any note.

The G5 chord Tabs

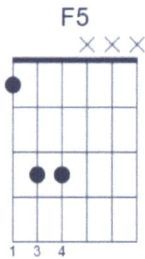

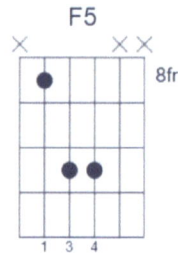

F5
× × ×

1 3 4

F5
×   × ×
8fr

1 3 4

Chord inversions

1. Consist of 3 notes;
2. They work for major and minor chords;
3. Each chord has two inversions;
4. Ex: C/E is E-G-C and C/G is G-C-E
5. Formula can be used on any note.

Chord inversions Tabs

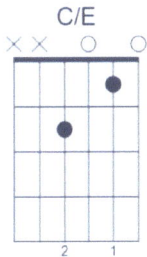

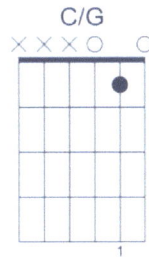

C/E

C/G

6th Chords

Major 6th chords

1. Consist of 4 notes;

2. Intervals between notes: M3, m3, M2;

3. M3/m3 = major/minor 3rd, M2 = major 2nd;

4. Ex: C6 is C–E–G–A;

5. Formula can be used on any note.

The C6 chord Tabs

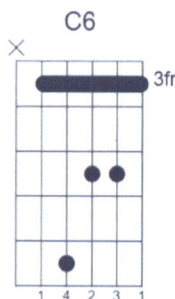

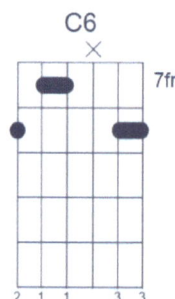

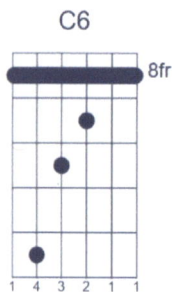

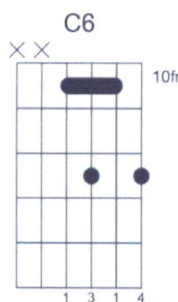

C6

C6   3fr

C6   7fr

C6   8fr

C6   10fr

Minor 6th chords

1. Consist of 4 notes;
2. Intervals between notes: m3, M3, M2;
3. M3/m3 = major/minor 3rd, M2 = major 2nd;
4. Ex: Cm6 is C–Eb–G–A;
5. Formula can be used on any note.

The Cm6 chord Tabs

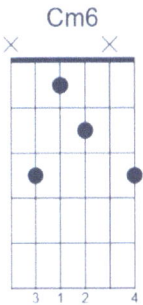

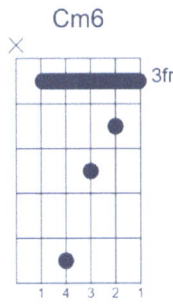

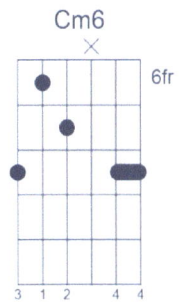

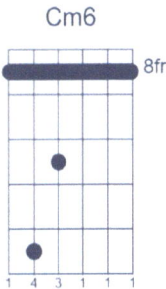

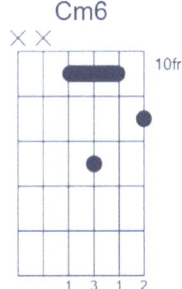

Augmented 6th chords

1. Consist of 4 notes;
2. Intervals between notes: M3, M3, m2;
3. M3 = major 3rd, m2 = minor 2nd;
4. Ex: Caug6 is C–E–G#–A;
5. Formula can be used on any note.

The Caug6 chord Tabs

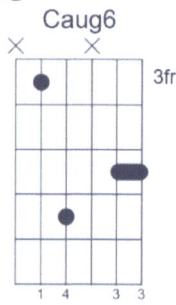

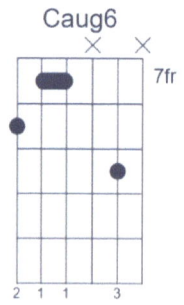

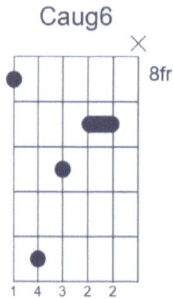

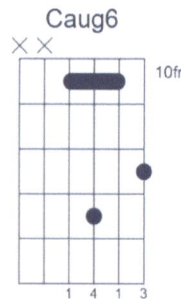

Caug6

Caug6   3fr

Caug6   7fr

Caug6   8fr

Caug6   10fr

Added Tone Chords

Major add9 chords

1. Consist of 4 notes;

2. Intervals between notes: M3, m3, P5;

3. M3/m3 = major/minor 3rd, P5 = perfect 5th

4. Ex: Cadd9 is C–E–G–D;

5. Formula can be used on any note.

The Cadd9 chord Tabs

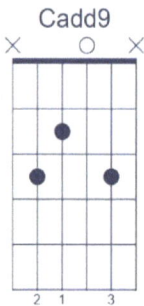

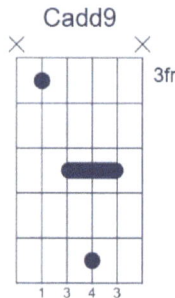

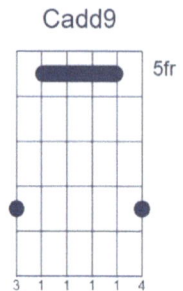

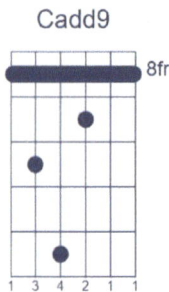

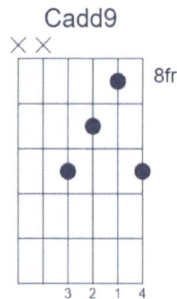

Cadd9

×   ○   ×

2 1 3

Cadd9

×   ×   3fr

1 3 4 3

Cadd9

5fr

3 1 1 1 1 4

Cadd9

8fr

1 3 4 2 1 1

Cadd9

× × 8fr

3 2 1 4

32

Minor add9 chords

1. Consist of 4 notes;
2. Intervals between notes: m3, M3, P5;
3. M3/m3 = major/minor 3rd, P5 = perfect 5th;
4. Ex: Cmadd9 is C–Eb–G–D;
5. Formula can be used on any note.

The Cmadd9 chord Tabs

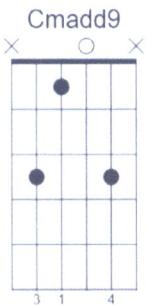

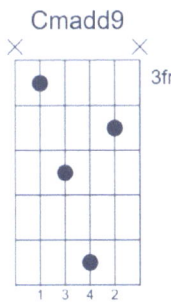

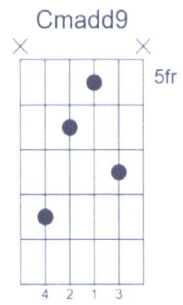

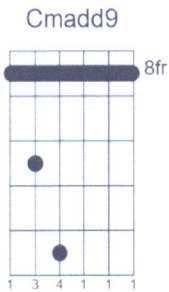

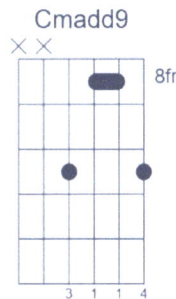

Cmadd9

Cmadd9   3fr

Cmadd9   5fr

Cmadd9   8fr

Cmadd9   8fr

Major add11 chords

1. Consist of 4 notes;
2. Intervals between notes: M3, m3, m7;
3. M3/m3 = major/minor 3rd, m7 = minor 7th;
4. Ex: Dadd11 is D–F#–A–G;
5. Formula can be used on any note.

The Dadd11 chord Tabs

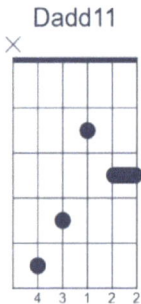

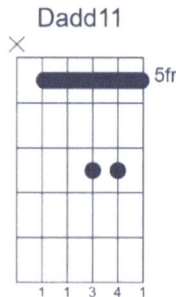

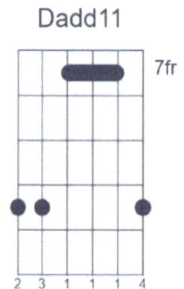

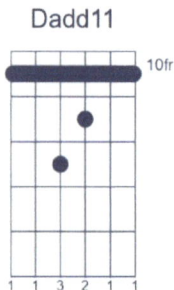

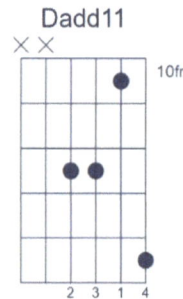

Dadd11

Dadd11

Dadd11

Dadd11

Dadd11

Minor add11 chords

1. Consist of 4 notes;
2. Intervals between notes: m3, M3, m7;
3. M3/m3 = major/minor 3rd, m7 = minor 7th;
4. Ex: Dmadd11 is D-F-A-G;
5. Formula can be used on any note.

The Dmadd11 chord Tabs

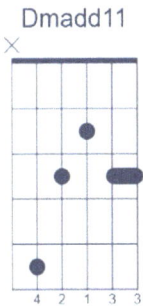

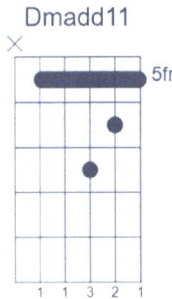

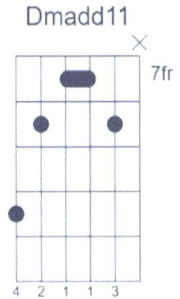

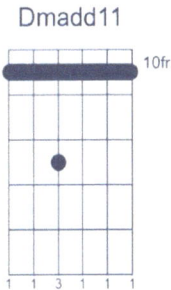

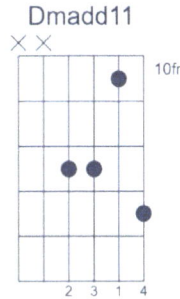

Dmadd11

Dmadd11
5fr

Dmadd11
7fr

Dmadd11
10fr

Dmadd11
10fr

Major 9th chords

1. **Consist of 5 notes;**

2. **Intervals between notes: M3, m3, M3, m3;**

3. **M3 = major 3rd, m3 = minor 3rd;**

4. **Ex: Cmaj9 is C–E–G–B–D;**

5. **Formula can be used on any note.**

The Cmaj9 chord Tabs

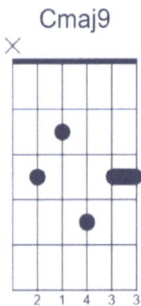

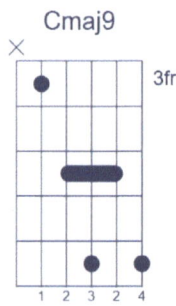

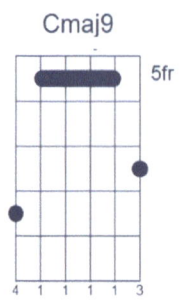

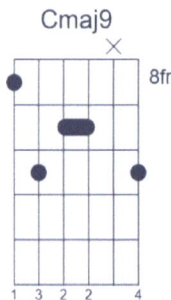

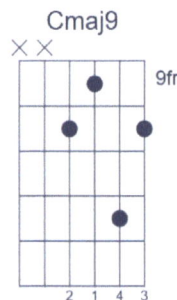

Cmaj9

Cmaj9

Cmaj9

Cmaj9

Cmaj9

Dominant 9th chords

1. Consist of 5 notes;

2. Intervals between notes: M3, m3, m3, M3;

3. M3 = major 3rd, m3 = minor 3rd;

4. Ex: C9 is C–E–G–Bb–D;

5. Formula can be used on any note.

The C9 chord Tabs

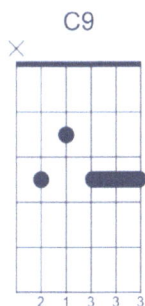

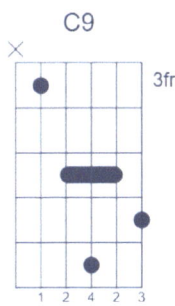

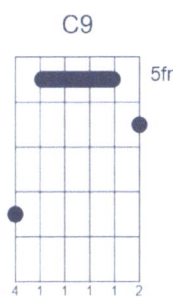

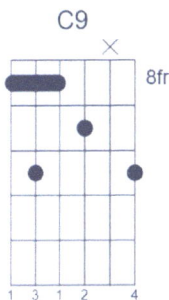

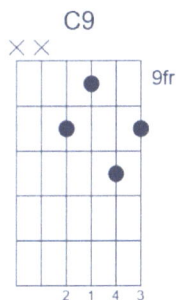

Minor 9th chords

1. Consist of 5 notes;
2. Intervals between notes: m3, M3, m3, M3;
3. M3 = major 3rd, m3 = minor 3rd;
4. Ex: Cm9 is C–Eb–G–Bb–D;
5. Formula can be used on any note.

The Cm9 chord Tabs

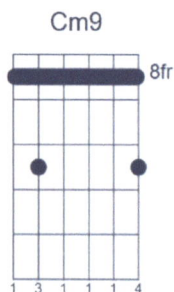

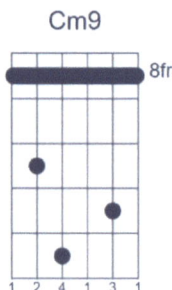

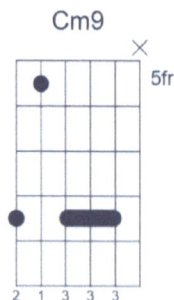

Cm9

Cm9

Cm9

Cm9

Minor 9th(b5) chords

1. Consist of 5 notes;
2. Intervals between notes: m3, m3, M3, M3;
3. M3 = major 3rd, m3 = minor 3rd;
4. Ex: Cm9(b5) is C-Eb-Gb-Bb-D;
5. Formula can be used on any note.

The Cm9(b5) chord Tabs

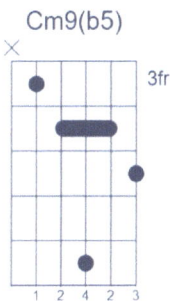

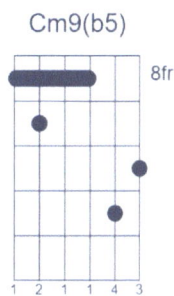

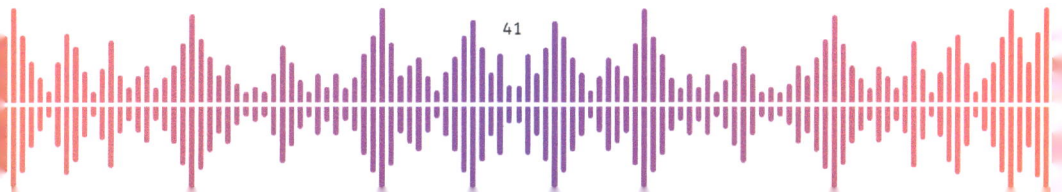

Cm9(b5)

3fr

1 2 4 2 3

Cm9(b5)

8fr

1 2 1 1 4 3

11th Chords

Major 11th chords

1. Consist of 6 notes;
2. Intervals between notes: M3, m3, M3, m3, m3;
3. M3 = major 3rd, m3 = minor 3rd;
4. Ex: Cmaj11 is C–E–G–B–D–F;
5. Formula can be used on any note.

The Cmaj11 chord Tabs

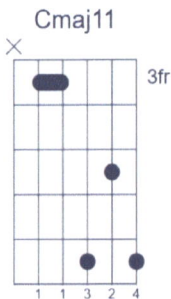

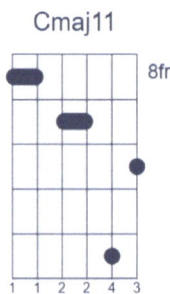

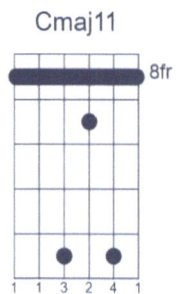

Cmaj11

3fr

1 1 3 2 4

Cmaj11

8fr

1 1 2 2 4 3

Cmaj11

8fr

1 1 3 2 4 1

Dominant 11th chords

1. Consist of 6 notes;

2. Intervals between notes: M3, m3, m3, M3, m3;

3. M3 = major 3rd, m3 = minor 3rd;

4. Ex: C11 is C–E–G–Bb–D–F;

5. Formula can be used on any note.

The C11 chord Tabs

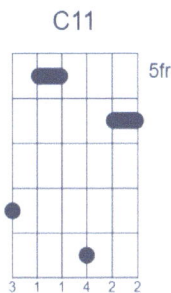

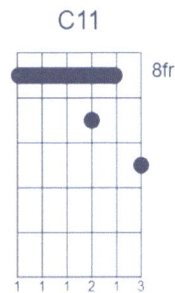

C11

5fr

3 1 1 4 2 2

C11

8fr

1 1 1 2 1 3

Minor 11th chords

1. Consist of 6 notes;
2. Intervals between notes: m3, M3, m3, M3, m3;
3. M3 = major 3rd, m3 = minor 3rd;
4. Ex: Cm11 is C–Eb–G–Bb–D–F;
5. Formula can be used on any note.

The Cm11 chord Tabs

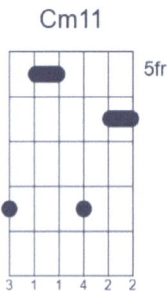

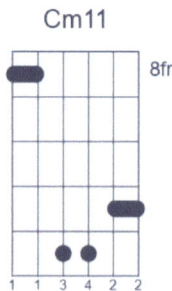

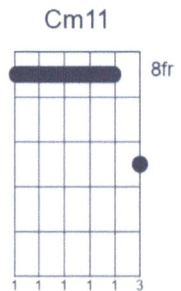

Cm11 — 5fr

Cm11 — 8fr

Cm11 — 8fr

Minor 11th(b5) chords

1. Consist of 6 notes;
2. Intervals between notes: m3, m3, M3, M3, m3;
3. M3 = major 3rd, m3 = minor 3rd;
4. Ex: Cm11(b5) is C–Eb–Gb–Bb–D–F;
5. Formula can be used on any note.

The Cm11(b5) chord Tab

Cm11(b5)

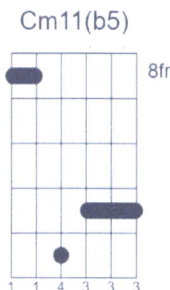

8fr

1 1 4 3 3 3

13th Chords

Major 13th chords

1. Consist of 7 notes;
2. Intervals: M3, m3, M3, m3, m3, M3;
3. M3 = major 3rd, m3 = minor 3rd;
4. Ex: Cmaj13 is C–E–G–B–D–F–A;
5. Formula can be used on any note.

The Cmaj13 chord Tab

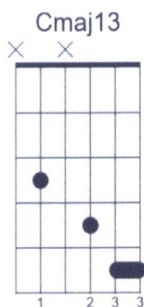

Cmaj13

Dominant 13th chords

1. Consist of 7 notes;
2. Intervals: M3, m3, m3, M3, m3, M3;
3. M3 = major 3rd, m3 = minor 3rd;
4. Ex: C13 is C–E–G–Bb–D–F–A;
5. Formula can be used on any note.

The C13 chord Tab

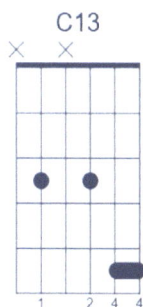

C13

Minor 13th chords

1. Consist of 7 notes;
2. Intervals: m3, M3, m3, M3, m3, M3;
3. M3 = major 3rd, m3 = minor 3rd;
4. Ex: Cm13 is C–Eb–G–Bb–D–F–A;
5. Formula can be used on any note.

The Cm13 chord Tab

Cm13

Minor 13th(b5) chords

1. Consist of 7 notes;
2. Intervals: m3, m3, M3, M3, m3, M3;
3. M3 = major 3rd, m3 = minor 3rd;
4. Ex: Cm13(b5) is C–Eb–Gb–Bb–D–F–A;
5. Formula can be used on any note.

The Cm13(b5) chord Tab

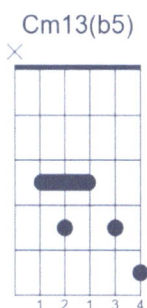

Cm13(b5)

Chord Equivalencies

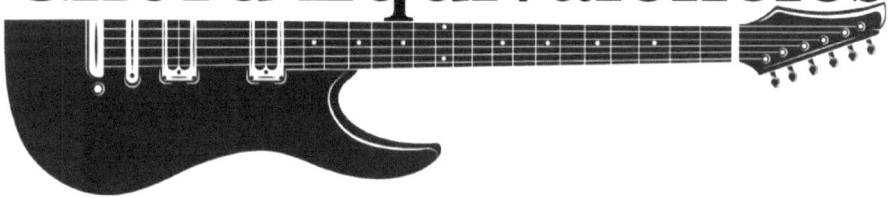

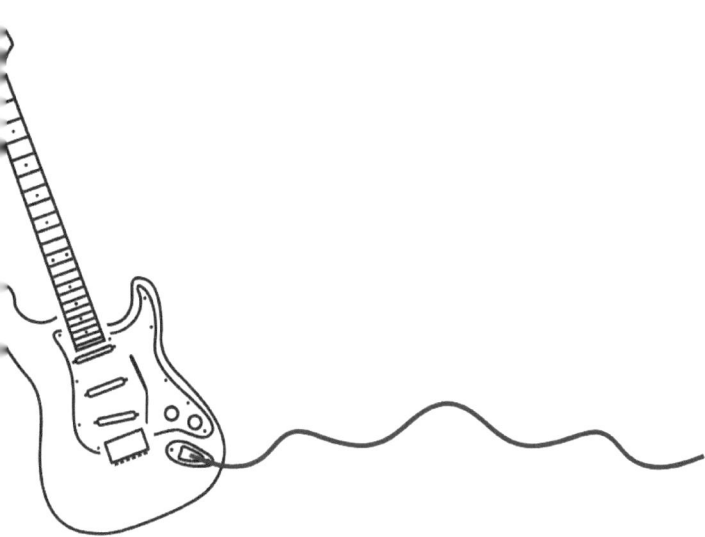

Diminished 6th chords have the same forms as **diminished 7th chords**; hence, there isn't a dedicated chapter for them.

The same logic applies for **add13 chords**. Such chords are identical with **major 6th chords** on the guitar, so that is why there is no dedicated chapter for them either.

www.ingramcontent.com/pod-product-compliance
Lightning Source LLC
LaVergne TN
LVHW010022070426
835508LV00001B/12